Timeless baby blankets

The Best of Mary Maxim®

LEISURE ARTS, INC. • Maumelle, Arkansas

Cozy Mariner's Blanket

■■■□ INTERMEDIATE

SHOPPING LIST

Yarn (Worsted Weight)
Mary Maxim Starlette
[3.5 ounces, 180 yards
(100 grams, 165 meters) per ball]:
- ☐ Main Color - Dk Blue 3 balls
- ☐ Contrast Color - Lt Blue 3 balls

Knitting Needles
32" (80 cm) Circular Needle
- ☐ Size 8 (5 mm)
    or size needed for gauge

Additional Supplies
- ☐ Markers - 4

SIZE INFORMATION
Finished: 34" x 37" [86.5 x 94 cm]

GAUGE INFORMATION
16 sts and 23 rows to 4" [10 cm] measured over Contrast Color block and 18 sts and 23 rows to 4" [10 cm] measured over Main Color block, using the **suggested** needle or any size needle which will give the correct stitch gauge or tension.

TO SAVE TIME, TAKE TIME TO CHECK GAUGE

STITCH GUIDE
C2B - Cable 2 Back: K2tog, do not drop from left needle, but insert right needle through 1st st and knit it again, then drop both sts from left needle.
SKP - Slip 1, knit 1, pass slipped stitch over knit 1.

Note: The Rope pattern blocks will pull in and be narrower than the other pattern blocks. To compensate for this, once the blanket has been completed, we suggest blocking, or washing the finished work. Instructions are included at the end of the pattern.

INSTRUCTIONS

Anchor Pattern: (Using CC, worked over 28 sts)
Row 1: (right side) Knit.
Row 2: Purl.
Rows 3-6: Repeat Rows 1 and 2 twice.
Row 7: Knit.
Row 8: P 13, k2, p 13.
Row 9: K 11, p2, C2B, p2, k 11.
Row 10: P 10, [k2, p1] twice, k2, p 10.
Row 11: K9, p2, k2, C2B, k2, p2, k9.
Row 12: P8, [k2, p3] twice, k2, p8.
Row 13: K7, k1 tbl, p2, k3, C2B, k3, p2, k1 tbl, k7.
Row 14: P8, k1, p4, k2, p4, k1, p8.
Rows 15, 17 and 19: K 13, C2B, k 13.
Rows 16 and 18: P 13, k2, p 13.
Row 20: P 11, k6, p 11.
Row 21: K 10, k1 tbl, p6, k1 tbl, k 10.
Row 22: P 13, k2, p 13.
Rows 23-26: Repeat Rows 15 and 16 twice.
Row 27: K 11, k1 tbl, p4, k1 tbl, k 11.
Row 28: P 11, k2, p2, k2, p 11.
Row 29: K 10, k1 tbl, p2, k2, p2, k1 tbl, k 10.
Row 30: P 12, k4, p 12.
Row 31: K 12, k1 tbl, p2, k1 tbl, k 12.
Row 32: Purl.
Rows 33-38: Repeat Rows 1 and 2 three times.

Boat Pattern: (Using CC, worked over 28 sts)
Row 1: (right side) Knit.
Row 2: Purl.
Rows 3-10: Repeat Rows 1 and 2 four times.
Row 11: K9, p 10, k9.
Row 12: P8, k 12, p8.
Row 13: K7, p 14, k7.
Row 14: Purl.
Row 15: Knit.
Row 16: P6, k6, p1, k9, p6.
Row 17: K7, p8, k1 tbl, p6, k6.
Row 18: P6, k6, p1, k8, p7.
Row 19: K8, p7, k1 tbl, p5, k7.
Row 20: P7, k5, p1, k6, p9.
Row 21: K9, p6, k1 tbl, p4, k8.
Row 22: P8, k4, p1, k5, p 10.
Row 23: K 11, p4, k1 tbl, p3, k9.

3

Row 24: P9, k3, p1, k4, p 11.
Row 25: K 12, p3, k1 tbl, p2, k 10.
Row 26: P 10, k2, p1, k2, p 13.
Row 27: K 13, p2, k1 tbl, p1, k 11.
Row 28: P 13, k1, p 14.
Row 29: Knit.
Row 30: Purl.
Rows 31-38: Repeat Rows 29 and 30 four times.

Rope Pattern: (Using MC, worked over 28 sts)
Row 1: (right side) Knit.
Row 2: K1, [p2, k2] 6 times, p2, k1.
Row 3: P1, [C2B, p2] 6 times, C2B, p1.
Row 4: K1, [p2, k2] 6 times, p2, k1.
Rows 5-38: Repeat Rows 3 and 4.

To Make:
Border: Using MC, cast on 147 sts. Do not join, but work back and forth as follows:
Row 1: (wrong side) P1, *k1, p1; rep from * to end.
Row 2: SKP, k to last 2 sts, k2tog - 145 sts.
Row 3: Knit.
Rows 4-7: Repeat Rows 2 and 3 twice - 141 sts at end of Row 7.
Row 8: SKP, k to end - 140 sts.
Row 9: Knit.

First Row: Set patterns in place as follows:
Row 1: Using CC, work Row 1 of Anchor Pattern over first 28 sts, place a marker, using MC, work Row 1 of Rope Pattern over next 28 sts, place a marker, join another ball of CC and work Row 1 of Boat Pattern over next 28 sts, place a marker, join another ball of MC and work Row 1 of Rope Pattern over next 28 sts, place a marker, join another ball of CC and work Row 1 of Anchor Pattern over last 28 sts.
Row 2: Using CC, work Row 2 of Anchor Pattern to first marker, sl marker, using MC, work Row 2 of Rope Pattern to next marker, sl marker, using CC, work Row 2 of Boat Pattern to next marker, sl marker, using MC, work Row 2 of Rope Pattern to next marker, sl marker, using CC, work Row 2 of Anchor Pattern to end.
Patterns are now set in place. Continue until 38 rows have been completed.
Second Row: Set patterns in place as follows:
Row 1: Using MC, work Row 1 of Rope Pattern to first marker, sl marker, using CC, work Row 1 of Boat Pattern to next marker, sl marker, join another ball of MC and work Row 1 of Rope Pattern to next marker, sl marker, join another ball of CC and work Row 1 of Boat Pattern to next marker, sl marker, join another ball of MC and work Row 1 of Rope Pattern to end.

Row 2: Using MC, work Row 2 of Rope Pattern to first marker, sl marker, using CC, work Row 2 of Boat Pattern to next marker, sl marker, using MC, work Row 2 of Rope Pattern to next marker, sl marker, using CC, work Row 2 of Boat Pattern to next marker, sl marker, using MC, work Row 2 of Rope Pattern to end.
Patterns are now set in place. Continue until 38 rows have been completed.
Third Row: Set patterns in place as follows:
Row 1: Using CC, work Row 1 of Boat Pattern to first marker, sl marker, using MC, work Row 1 of Rope Pattern to next marker, sl marker, join another ball of CC and work Row 1 of Anchor Pattern to next marker, sl marker, join another ball of MC and work Row 1 of Rope Pattern to next marker, sl marker, join another ball of CC and work Row 1 of Boat Pattern to end.
Row 2: Using CC, work Row 2 of Boat Pattern to first marker, sl marker, using MC, work Row 2 of Rope Pattern to next marker, sl marker, using CC, work Row 2 of Anchor Pattern to next marker, sl marker, using MC, work Row 2 of Rope Pattern to next marker, sl marker, using CC, work Row 2 of Boat Pattern to end.
Patterns are now set in place. Continue until 38 rows have been completed.

Placement Diagram

CC Anchor	MC Rope	**CC Boat**	MC Rope	**CC Anchor**
MC Rope	**CC Boat**	MC Rope	**CC Boat**	MC Rope
CC Boat	MC Rope	**CC Anchor**	MC Rope	**CC Boat**
MC Rope	**CC Boat**	MC Rope	**CC Boat**	MC Rope
CC Anchor	MC Rope	**CC Boat**	MC Rope	**CC Anchor**

Fourth Row: Work as given for Second Row.

Fifth Row: Work as given for First Row.

Top Border:

Row 1: (right side) Using MC only, knit all sts, inc one st in center of row and removing markers - 141 sts.

Row 2: Knit.

Row 3: K1, inc one st in next st, k to last 2 sts, inc one st in next st, k1 - 143 sts.

Row 4: Knit.

Rows 5 and 7: Repeat Row 3 - 147 sts at end of Row 7.

Rows 6 and 8: Knit.

Row 9: K1, *p1, k1; rep from * to end. Cast off in pattern.

Side Borders: Using MC, with right side of blanket facing, pick up and k 141 sts evenly across one side edge.

Beg with Row 2, complete as given for Top Border.

Repeat on opposite side.

Sew each corner closed.

Weave in all ends.

To Block: Pin blanket out on a flat surface so that all blocks are neat and even. Cover with fairly damp towels or a sheet. Apply pressure over the entire surface of the blanket then leave until towels or sheet are dry. Remove the towels or sheet and leave blanket to dry.

Or, if desired, wash the blanket on its own, using cool water and delicate cycle. Place in the dryer for a maximum of 5 minutes on a low heat setting. Remove and lay out flat to finish drying.

Design by Vera Shoemaker.

Mitered Eyelet Blanket

INTERMEDIATE

SHOPPING LIST

Yarn (Light Weight)

Mary Maxim Sugar Baby Stripes
[3.5 ounces, 295 yards
(100 grams, 269 meters) per ball]:
☐ 4 balls

Knitting Needles
☐ Size 9 (5.5 mm)
or size needed for gauge

SIZE INFORMATION
Finished: 30" x 40" [76 x 101.5 cm]

GAUGE INFORMATION
One motif is 10" [25.5 cm] x 10" [25.5 cm] when measured diagonally from corner to corner, using the **suggested** needles or any size needles which will give the correct stitch gauge.

TO SAVE TIME, TAKE TIME TO CHECK GAUGE

STITCH GUIDE

DD - double decrease: Slip next 2 stitches to right needle at the same time (as if to k2tog), k1 from left needle, then pass both slipped stitches over k1 at the same time.

W&T - Wrap and Turn: Bring yarn forward as if to purl, slip next stitch to right needle then take yarn to back and slip the same stitch back to left needle and turn work. Do not worry about working the wrap tog with the stitch on the return rows as it will not be visible within the Garter st.

INSTRUCTIONS

Basic Motif: Cast on 61 sts loosely.
Row 1: (wrong side) Knit.
Row 2: K 29, DD, k 29 - 59 sts.
Row 3: Purl.
Row 4: K 28, DD, k 28 - 57 sts.
Row 5: K 28, p1, k 28.
Row 6: K 27, DD, k 27 - 55 sts.
Row 7: P2, [p2tog, yrn, p3] 5 times, p1, [p3, yrn, p2tog] 5 times, p2.
Row 8: K 26, DD, k 26 - 53 sts.
Row 9: K 26, p1, k 26.
Row 10: K 25, DD, k 25 - 51 sts.
Row 11: Purl.
Row 12: K 24, DD, k 24 - 49 sts.
Row 13: K 24, p1, k 24.
Row 14: K 23, DD, k 23 - 47 sts.
Row 15: P3, [p2tog, yrn, p3] 4 times, p1, [p3, yrn, p2tog] 4 times, p3.
Row 16: K 22, DD, k 22 - 45 sts.
Row 17: K 22, p1, k 22.
Row 18: K 21, DD, k 21 - 43 sts.
Row 19: Purl.
Row 20: K 20, DD, k 20 - 41 sts.
Row 21: K 20, p1, k 20.
Row 22: K 19, DD, k 19 - 39 sts.
Row 23: K 19, p1, k 19.
Row 24: K 18, DD, k 18 - 37 sts.
Row 25: K 18, p1, k 18.
Row 26: K 17, DD, k 17 - 35 sts.
Row 27: K 17, p1, k 17.
Row 28: K 16, DD, k 16 - 33 sts.
Row 29: K 16, p1, k 16.
Row 30: K 15, DD, k 15 - 31 sts.
Row 31: K 15, p1, k 15.
Row 32: K 14, DD, k 14 - 29 sts.
Row 33: K 14, p1, k 14.
Row 34: K 13, DD, k 13 - 27 sts.
Row 35: K 13, p1, k 13.
Row 36: K 12, DD, k 12 - 25 sts.
Row 37: K 12, p1, k 12.
Row 38: K 11, DD, k 11 - 23 sts.
Row 39: K 11, p1, k 11.
Row 40: K 10 , DD, k 10 - 21 sts.
Row 41: K 10, p1, k 10.
Row 42: K9, DD, k9 - 19 sts.
Row 43: K9, p1, k9.
Row 44: K8, DD, k8 - 17 sts.

Due to the nature of this yarn, each Blanket will have its own unique color sequence.

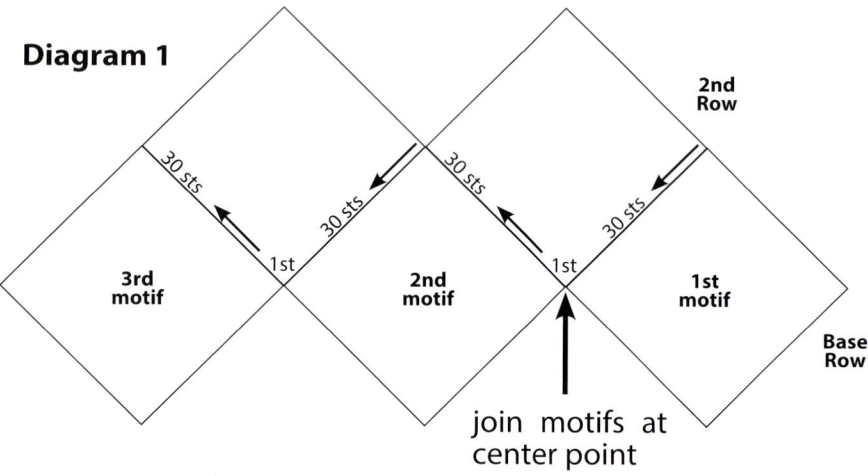

Diagram 1

join motifs at center point

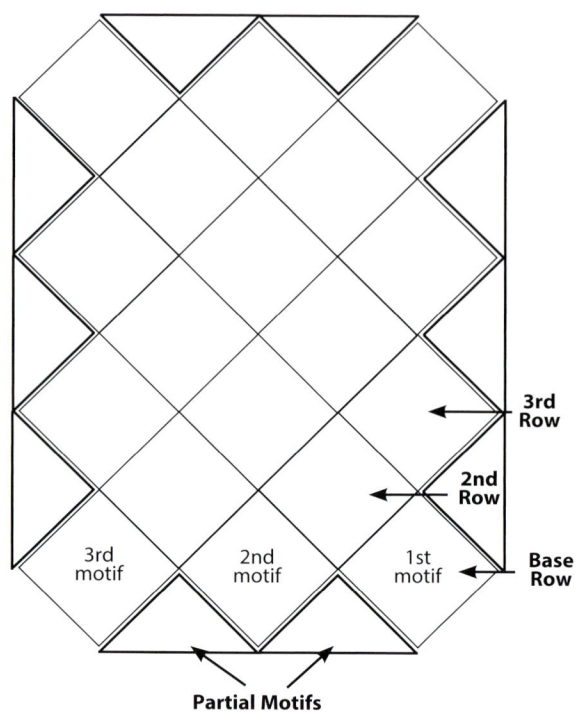

Assembly Diagram

Partial Motifs

Row 45: K8, p1, k8.
Row 46: K7, DD, k7 - 15 sts.
Row 47: K7, p1, k7.
Row 48: K6, DD, k6 - 13 sts.
Row 49: K6, p1, k6.
Row 50: K5, DD, k5 - 11 sts.
Row 51: K5, p1, k5.
Row 52: K4, DD, k4 - 9 sts.
Row 53: K4, p1, k4.
Row 54: K3, DD, k3 - 7 sts.
Row 55: K3, p1, k3.
Row 56: K2, DD, k2 - 5 sts.
Row 57: K2, p1, k2.
Row 58: K1, DD, k1 - 3 sts.
Row 59: P3tog. Fasten off.
Repeat these 59 rows for each motif.

Base Row: Work 3 Basic Motifs. Once all 3 motifs have been completed, lay motifs side by side, with right sides upwards and join together at center point. (see Diagram 1)

Second Row: With right side facing, beg at point of 1st Motif, pick up and k 30 sts down side to join, pick up and k1 st at join, then pick up and k 30 sts up side of 2nd Motif to point - 61 sts. Work Rows 1-59 of Basic Motif. With right side facing, pick up and k 61 sts along Motifs 2 and 3 as for previous motif and work Rows 1-59 of Basic Motif.

Third Row:
Make a first motif as follows:
Cast on 30 sts, with right side facing, pick up and k1 st in corner of first motif of Second Row, then pick up and k 30 sts along side to point of same motif - 61 sts.
Work Rows 1-59 of Basic Motif.
Now work the next motif as in Second Row.
Now make the last motif as follows:
With right side facing, pick up and k 30 sts along side of last motif to center point, pick up and k1 at center point, then cast on 30 sts - 61 sts.
Work Rows 1-59 of Basic Motif.

www.leisurearts.com

A closer view of the Partial Motifs that finish the blanket

Now rep Second and Third Rows twice more.
There will be 4 rows of three motifs and 3 rows of two motifs once the Blanket has been completed.
Weave in all ends.

Partial Motifs:
Worked in "V's" around outside edge of blanket (see Assembly Diagram). With right side facing, beg at point of 1st Motif, pick up and k 30 sts down side to join, pick up and k1 st at join, then pick up and k 30 sts up side of 2nd Motif to point - 61 sts.
Next Row: (wrong side) Knit.

Now work short rows of Garter st as follows:
Row 1: K 29, DD, k1, W&T.
Row 2: K1, p1, k2, W&T.
Row 3: K7, W&T.
Row 4: K4, p1, k4, W&T.
Row 5: K3, DD, k6, W&T.
Row 6: K6, p1, k6, W&T.
Row 7: K 16, W&T.
Row 8: K9, p1, k9, W&T.
Row 9: K8, DD, k 11, W&T.
Row 10: K 11, p1, k 11, W&T.
Row 11: K 26, W&T.
Row 12: K 14, p1, k 14, W&T.
Row 13: K 13, DD, k 16, W&T.
Row 14: K 16, p1, k 16, W&T.
Row 15: K 36, W&T.
Row 16: K 19, p1, k 19, W&T.
Row 17: K 18, DD, k 21, W&T.
Row 18: K 21, p1, k 21, W&T.
Row 19: K 46, W&T.
Row 20: K 24, p1, k 24, W&T.
Row 21: K 23, DD, k 24.
Row 22: Cast off knitwise, slipping the first st and k2tog over last 2 sts, then pass the last st over. Fasten off.
Repeat Partial Motif around outside edge of blanket as indicated in Assembly Diagram.
Weave in all ends.

Honeycomb Blanket

INTERMEDIATE

SHOPPING LIST

Yarn (Dk/Sport Weight)

Mary Maxim Baby's Best
[1.75 ounces, 171 yards (50 grams, 156 meters) per ball]:

- ☐ Main Color - Mint   4 balls
- ☐ Contrast Color - Rainbow Print   3 balls

Knitting Needles

32" [80 cm] Circular Needle
- ☐ Size 6 (4 mm)
  or size needed for gauge

SIZE INFORMATION

Finished: 28" x 33¼" [71 x 84.5 cm]

GAUGE INFORMATION

24 sts and 40 rows to 4" [10 cm] measured over pattern, using **suggested** needle or any size needle which will give the correct gauge.

TO SAVE TIME, TAKE TIME TO CHECK GAUGE

INSTRUCTIONS

Note: On wrong side rows, slip all sts knitwise with yarn held in front of work. On right side rows, slip all sts purlwise with yarn held in back of work.

With CC, cast on 148 sts loosely.
Row 1: (right side) Purl.
Rows 2 and 3: Knit.
Row 4: Using MC, p1, sl 2, *p6, sl 2; rep from * to last st, p1.
Row 5: K1, sl 2, *k6, sl 2; rep from * to last st, k1.
Rows 6-9: Repeat Rows 4 and 5 twice.
Rows 10 and 11: Using CC, purl.
Rows 12 and 13: Knit.
Row 14: Using MC, p5, sl 2, *p6, sl 2; rep from * to last 5 sts, p5.
Row 15: K5, sl 2, *k6, sl 2; rep from * to last 5 sts, k5.
Rows 16-19: Repeat Rows 14 and 15 twice.
Rows 20 and 21: Using CC, purl.
Rows 22 and 23: Knit.
Repeat Rows 4-23 until blanket measures about 30" [76 cm] from cast on edge.
Change to MC and purl one row, inc one st in center - 149 sts. Do not cast off.

Top Border:
Now using MC only, continue as follows:
Row 1: (right side) P1, k3, *p3, k3; rep from * to last st, p1.
Row 2: Knit into front and back (kf&b) of first st, p3, *k3, p3; rep from * to last st, kf&b.
Row 3: P2, k3, *p3, k3; rep from * to last 2 sts, p2.
Row 4: K1, kf&b, p3, *k3, p3; rep from * to last 2 sts, kf&b, k1.
Row 5: *P3, k3; rep from * to last 3 sts, p3.
Row 6: K1, kf&b, k1, p3, *k3, p3; rep from * to last 3 sts, k1, kf&b, k1.
Row 7: P4, k3, *p3, k3; rep from * to last 4 sts, p4.
Row 8: K4, p3, *k3, p3; rep from * to last 4 sts, k4.
Repeat these last 2 rows 4 times more. Cast off in pattern.

Bottom Border: Using MC, with wrong side facing, pick up and p 149 sts evenly across cast on edge. Work as given for Top Border.

Side Borders: Using MC, with wrong side facing, pick up and p 173 sts evenly across one side of blanket. Now work as given for Top Border. Repeat for 2nd side.
Sew corners neatly.
Weave in all ends.

Cable Patches Blanket

INTERMEDIATE

SHOPPING LIST

Yarn (Worsted Weight)

Mary Maxim Marbles
[3.5 ounces, 218 yards
(100 grams, 199 meters) per ball]:
☐ Watermelon   5 balls

Knitting Needles
36" (90 cm) Circular Needle
☐ Size 9 (5.5 mm)
or size needed for gauge

Additional Supplies
☐ Cable needle

SIZE INFORMATION
Finished: 29" x 36" [73.5 x 91.5 cm]

GAUGE INFORMATION
16 sts and 23 rows to 4" [10 cm] measured over Stocking stitch, using **suggested** needle or any size needle which will give the correct gauge.

TO SAVE TIME, TAKE TIME TO CHECK GAUGE

STITCH GUIDE

C8B - Cable 8 Back: Slip next 4 sts onto cable needle and hold to back of work, k4 from left needle, then k4 from cable needle.

INSTRUCTIONS

Cast on 120 sts and knit 7 rows.
**Next Row: (inc row) K 24, *p2, [inc one st in next st knitwise] 4 times, p2, k 24; rep from * to end - 132 sts.

Now work Stripe A as follows:
Row 1: (wrong side) K7, p 17, [k2, p8, k2, p 24] twice, k2, p8, k2, p 17, k7.
Row 2: K 24, *p2, k8, p2, k 24; rep from * to end.
Row 3: As Row 1.
Row 4: As Row 2.
Row 5: As Row 1.
Row 6: As Row 2.
Row 7: As Row 1.
Row 8: K 24, *p2, C8B, p2, k 24; rep from * to end.
Repeat these 8 rows for pattern 3 times more, then Rows 1-4 once.
Next Row: (dec row) K 26, *[k2tog] 4 times, k 28; rep from * once more, [k2tog] 4 times, k 26 - 120 sts.
Knit 5 rows. **#**

Now work Stripe B as follows:
Next Row: (inc row) K 13, [inc one st in next st knitwise] 4 times, *k 26, [inc one st in next st knitwise] 4 times; rep from * twice more, k 13 - 136 sts.
Row 1: (right side) K 11, *p2, k8, p2, k 22; rep from * twice more, p2, k8, p2, k 11.
Row 2: K7, p4, *k2, p8, k2, p 22; rep from * twice more, k2, p8, k2, p4, k7.
Row 3: As Row 1.
Row 4: As Row 2.
Row 5: As Row 1.
Row 6: As Row 2.
Row 7: K 11, *p2, C8B, p2, k 22; rep from * twice more, p2, C8B, p2, k 11.
Row 8: As Row 2.
Repeat these 8 rows for pattern, 3 times more, then Rows 1-5 once.

Next Row: (dec row) K 13, *[k2tog] 4 times, k 26; rep from * twice more, [k2tog] 4 times, k 13 - 120 sts.
Knit 6 rows. ******

Now rep from ** to ** once, then rep from ** to # once more.
Knit one more row.
Cast off knitwise.
Weave in all ends.

Baby Entrelac Blanket

■■■▢ INTERMEDIATE

SHOPPING LIST

Yarn (Sport Weight)

Mary Maxim Baby Ragg
[1.75 ounces, 180 yards
(50 grams, 165 meters) per ball]:
- Color 1 - Mint Ragg   4 balls
- Color 2 - Lilac Ragg   5 balls

Knitting Needles
- Size 6 (4 mm)
  or size needed for gauge
  32" (80 cm) Circular Needle
- Size 7 (4.5mm)

SIZE INFORMATION

Finished: 34" x 43" [86.5 x 109 cm]

TO SAVE TIME, TAKE TIME TO CHECK GAUGE

GAUGE INFORMATION

22 sts and 28 rows to 4" [10 cm] measured over Stocking stitch using **suggested** smaller needles or any size needles which will give the correct gauge.

STITCH GUIDE

SSK - slip, slip, knit 2 together: Slip next 2 sts knitwise, one at a time, to right needle, insert left needle into fronts of these 2 sts and knit them together as usual.

SK2P - Slip one knitwise, knit next 2 sts together, pass slipped stitch over k2tog.

Note: Blanket is worked in connected triangles, then blocks as follows:

1) To begin, short rows are worked to create a beginning row of triangles.

2) A row of blocks is then worked between the triangles. Stitches are picked up along one edge of a triangle and a block is worked over these sts and at the same time, joined to the sts of one edge of the next triangle.

3) Each additional row of blocks is worked in the same way over previous rows of blocks.

4) Blanket is ended by working short rows to create a last row of triangles.

INSTRUCTIONS

Using smaller size needles and Color 1, cast on 152 sts and knit one row.

Beg Triangles: Make 13 triangles as follows:

Row 1: (right side) K2, turn.

Rows 2, 4, 6, 8, 10, 12 and 14: P to end of triangle, turn.

Row 3: K3, turn.

Row 5: K3, SSK, turn.

Row 7: K5, turn.

Row 9: K5, SSK, turn.

Row 11: K7, turn.

Row 13: K7, SSK, turn.

Row 15: K9, do not turn, (if needed, place a marker at end of Row 15 to indicate end of triangle).

Repeat these last 15 rows 11 times more.

Last Triangle: Repeat Rows 1-10.

Row 11: K4, k2tog, turn.

Rows 12 and 14: P to end of triangle, turn.

Row 13: K3, k2tog, turn.

Row 15: K2, k2tog, turn.

Row 16: (wrong side) SK2P, do not turn - one st remains on right needle.

First Row of Blocks

First Block: Change to Color 2. From wrong side, pick up and p8 sts evenly along edge of first triangle - 9 sts on right needle, turn.

Rows 1, 3, 5, 7, 9, 11, 13 and 15: K to end of block, turn.

Rows 2, 4, 6, 8, 10, 12 and 14: P8, p2tog (one st is Color 2, one st is Color 1), turn.

Row 16: P8, p3tog, do not turn.

Next Block: **From wrong side, pick up and p9 sts evenly spaced along edge of next triangle, turn.

Rows 1-16: Work Rows 1-16 of First Block.

Repeat from ** 10 times more.

Last Half Block: From wrong side, pick up and p9 sts evenly spaced along edge of last triangle, turn.

Rows 1, 3, 5, 7, 9, 11, 13 and 15: K to end of block, turn.

Rows 2, 4, 6, 8, 10, 12 and 14: P to last 2 sts, p2tog, turn.

Row 16: P2tog, turn.

Change to Color 1.

Row 17: (right side) K1, do not turn - one st remains on right needle.

#Second Row of Blocks

First Block: Using Color 1, from right side, pick up and k8 sts evenly along edge of first block - 9 sts on right needle, turn.

Rows 1, 3, 5, 7, 9, 11, 13 and 15: P to end of block, turn.

Rows 2, 4, 6, 8, 10, 12 and 14: K8, SSK, turn.

Row 16: K8, SK2P, place marker for end of block, do not turn.

Next Block: **From right side, pick up and k9 sts evenly spaced along edge of next block, turn.

Rows 1-16: Work Rows 1-16 of First Block.

Repeat from ** 10 times more.

Last Half Block: From right side, pick up and k9 sts evenly spaced along edge of last block, turn.

Rows 1, 3, 5, 7, 9, 11, 13 and 15: P to end of block, turn.

Rows 2, 4, 6, 8, 10, 12 and 14: K to last 2 sts, SSK, turn.

Row 16: SSK, turn.

Change to Color 2.

Row 17: (wrong side) P1, do not turn - one st on right needle.

Third Row of Blocks
First Block: Using Color 2, from wrong side, pick up and p8 sts evenly along edge of first block - 9 sts on right needle, turn.
Rows 1, 3, 5, 7, 9, 11, 13 and 15: K to end of block, turn.
Rows 2, 4, 6, 8, 10, 12 and 14: P8, p2tog, turn.
Row 16: P8, p3tog, turn, (if needed, place a marker at end of Row 15 to indicate end of block).
Next Block: **From wrong side, pick up and p9 sts evenly spaced along edge of next block, turn.
Rows 1-16: Work Rows 1-16 of First Block.
Repeat from ** 10 times more.
Last Half Block: From wrong side, pick up and p9 sts evenly spaced along edge of last block, turn.
Rows 1, 3, 5, 7, 9, 11, 13 and 15: K to end of block, turn.
Rows 2, 4, 6, 8, 10, 12 and 14: P to last 2 sts, p2tog, turn.
Row 16: P2tog, turn.
Change to Color 1.
Row 17: (right side) K1, do not turn - one st remains on right needle. #
Now rep from # to # for pattern 14 times more.

Last Row of Triangles: *Using Color 1, from right side, pick up and k8 sts evenly along edge of block - 9 sts, turn.
Rows 1, 3, 5, 7, 9, 11, 13 and 15: P to last 2 sts of triangle, p2tog, turn.
Rows 2, 4, 6, 8, 10, 12 and 14: K to last st of triangle, SSK, turn.
Row 16: SK2P, do not turn - one st remains on needle.
Repeat from * 15 times more.
Last Triangle: From right side, pick up and k8 sts evenly along edge of last block, turn.
Rows 1, 3, 5 and 7: P to last 2 sts of triangle, p2tog, turn.
Rows 2, 4, 6 and 8: K to last 2 sts of triangle, SSK, turn. At end of Row 8, one st rem. Fasten off.

Bottom Edging: Using circular needle, with right side facing, pick up and k 125 sts evenly spaced along bottom edge of blanket. Working in Garter st - every row knit, work as follows:
Row 1: (wrong side) Knit.
Row 2: K2, inc one st in next st, k to last 3 sts, inc one st in next st, k2.
Repeat these last 2 rows 4 times more, ending after a Row 2.
Cast off loosely knitwise.

Repeat on top edge of blanket.

Side Edging: Using circular needle, with right side facing, pick up and k 160 sts (10 sts evenly spaced along each side of block or triangle) along side edge of blanket. Work in Garter st as follows:
Row 1: (wrong side) Knit.
Row 2: K2, inc one st in next st, k to last 3 sts, inc one st in next st, k2.
Repeat these last 2 rows 4 times more, ending after a Row 2.
Cast off loosely knitwise.

To Complete: Weave in all ends. Sew mitered corners of edging together neatly.

Lace & Cables Blanket

INTERMEDIATE

SHOPPING LIST

Yarn (DK/Sport Weight)

Mary Maxim Baby's Best [1.75 ounces, 171 yards (50 grams, 157 meters) per ball]:

- ☐ Color 1 - Pink   3 balls
- ☐ Color 2 - White   3 balls
- ☐ Color 3 - Lavender   3 balls

Knitting Needles
- ☐ Size 6 (4 mm)

Additional Supplies
- ☐ Stitch markers

SIZE INFORMATION
Finished: 31 1/2" x 34 3/4" [80 x 88.5 cm]

GAUGE INFORMATION
Strip 1 = 4 1/2" [11.5 cm] wide, Strip 2 = 3 1/4" [8.25 cm] wide, both using the **suggested** needles or any size needles which will give the correct gauge.

TO SAVE TIME, TAKE TIME TO CHECK GAUGE

STITCH GUIDE

C4B - Cable 4 Back: Slip next 2 sts onto cable needle and hold to back of work, k2 from left needle, then k2 from cable needle.

SKP - Slip 1, knit 1, pass slipped stitch over knit 1.

SK2P - Slip 1, knit 2 together, pass slipped stitch over k2tog.

INSTRUCTIONS

Strip 1: Make 2 using Color 1, then 2 using Color 3.

Cast on 37 sts and work in pattern as follows:

Row 1: (right side) K1, p2, k4, p2, PM, k1, yo, SKP, p3, yo, SKP, k3, k2tog, yo, p3, k2tog, yo, k1, PM, p2, k4, p2, k1.

Row 2 and every alternate row following: K3, p4, k2, sl M, k the knit sts and p the purl sts and yo's as they appear across to next marker, sl M, k2, p4, k3.

Note: Slip markers on every row following.

Row 3: K1, p2, k4, p2, k1, yo, k1, SKP, p3, yo, SKP, k1, k2tog, yo, p3, k2tog, k1, yo, k1, p2, k4, p2, k1.

Row 5: K1, p2, C4B, p2, k1, yo, k2, SKP, p3, yo, SK2P, yo, p3, k2tog, k2, yo, k1, p2, C4B, p2, k1.

Row 7: K1, p2, k4, p2, k1, yo, k3, SKP, p7, k2tog, k3, yo, k1, p2, k4, p2, k1.

Row 9: K1, p2, k4, p2, k1, yo, k4, SKP, p5, k2tog, k4, yo, k1, p2, k4, p2, k1.

Row 11: K1, p2, C4B, p2, k1, yo, k5, SKP, p3, k2tog, k5, yo, k1, p2, C4B, p2, k1.

Row 13: K1, p2, k4, p2, k1, yo, k6, SKP, p1, k2tog, k6, yo, k1, p2, k4, p2, k1.

Row 15: K1, p2, k4, p2, k1, yo, k2, k2tog, yo, SKP, k2, p1, k2, k2tog, yo, SKP, k2, yo, k1, p2, k4, p2, k1.

Row 17: K1, p2, C4B, p2, k3, k2tog, yo, p1, yo, SKP, k1, p1, k1, k2tog, yo, p1, yo, SKP, k3, p2, C4B, p2, k1.

Row 19: K1, p2, k4, p2, k2, k2tog, yo, p3, yo, SKP, p1, k2tog, yo, p3, yo, SKP, k2, p2, k4, p2, k1.

Row 21: K1, p2, k4, p2, k1, k2tog, yo, p3, k2tog, [k1, yo] twice, k1, SKP, p3, yo, SKP, k1, p2, k4, p2, k1.

Row 23: K1, p2, C4B, p2, k2tog, yo, p3, k2tog, k2, yo, k1, yo, k2, SKP, p3, yo, SKP, p2, C4B, p2, k1.

Row 25: K1, p2, k4, p6, k2tog, k3, yo, k1, yo, k3, SKP, p6, k4, p2, k1.

Row 27: K1, p2, k4, p5, k2tog, k4, yo, k1, yo, k4, SKP, p5, k4, p2, k1.

Row 29: K1, p2, C4B, p4, k2tog, k5, yo, k1, yo, k5, SKP, p4, C4B, p2, k1.

Row 31: K1, p2, k4, p3, k2tog, k6, yo, k1, yo, k6, SKP, p3, k4, p2, k1.

Top

Row 33: K1, p2, k4, p3, k2, k2tog, yo, SKP, k2, yo, k1, yo, k2, k2tog, yo, SKP, k2, p3, k4, p2, k1.

Row 35: K1, p2, C4B, p3, k1, k2tog, yo, p1, yo, SKP, k5, k2tog, yo, p1, yo, SKP, k1, p3, C4B, p2, k1.

Row 36: Work as Row 2.

Repeat these 36 rows for pattern 7 times more, then rep Rows 1-6 once. Cast off.

Strip 2: Make 3 using Color 2.

Cast on 23 sts and work in pattern as follows:

Row 1: (right side) P2, k1, yo, SKP, p3, yo, SKP, k3, k2tog, yo, p3, k2tog, yo, k1, p2.

Row 2 and every alternate row following: K the knit sts and p the purl sts and yo's as they appear.

Row 3: P2, k1, yo, k1, SKP, p3, yo, SKP, k1, k2tog, yo, p3, k2tog, k1, yo, k1, p2.

Row 5: P2, k1, yo, k2, SKP, p3, yo, SK2P, yo, p3, k2tog, k2, yo, k1, p2.

Row 7: P2, k1, yo, k3, SKP, p7, k2tog, k3, yo, k1, p2.

Row 9: P2, k1, yo, k4, SKP, p5, k2tog, k4, yo, k1, p2.

Row 11: P2, k1, yo, k5, SKP, p3, k2tog, k5, yo, k1, p2.

Row 13: P2, k1, yo, k6, SKP, p1, k2tog, k6, yo, k1, p2.

Row 15: P2, k1, yo, k2, k2tog, yo, SKP, k2, p1, k2, k2tog, yo, SKP, k2, yo, k1, p2.

Row 17: P2, k3, k2tog, yo, p1, yo, SKP, k1, p1, k1, k2tog, yo, p1, yo, SKP, k3, p2.

Row 19: P2, k2, k2tog, yo, p3, yo, SKP, p1, k2tog, yo, p3, yo, SKP, k2, p2.

Row 21: P2, k1, k2tog, yo, p3, k2tog, [k1, yo] twice, k1, SKP, p3, yo, SKP, k1, p2.

Row 23: P2, k2tog, yo, p3, k2tog, k2, yo, k1, yo, k2, SKP, p3, yo, SKP, p2.

Row 25: P6, k2tog, k3, yo, k1, yo, k3, SKP, p6.

Row 27: P5, k2tog, k4, yo, k1, yo, k4, SKP, p5.

Row 29: P4, k2tog, k5, yo, k1, yo, k5, SKP, p4.

Row 31: P3, k2tog, k6, yo, k1, yo, k6, SKP, p3.

Row 33: P3, k2, k2tog, yo, SKP, k2, yo, k1, yo, k2, k2tog, yo, SKP, k2, p3.

Row 35: P3, k1, k2tog, yo, p1, yo, SKP, k5, k2tog, yo, p1, yo, SKP, k1, p3.

Row 36: Work as Row 2.

Repeat these 36 rows for pattern 7 times more, then rep Rows 1-6 once. Cast off.

To Assemble: Following Placement Diagram above, sew strips together neatly.

Placement Diagram

Pink Strip 1	White Strip 2	Lavender Strip 1	White Strip 2	Lavender Strip 1	White Strip 2	Pink Strip 1

General Instructions

ABBREVIATIONS

"	inches
approx.	approximately
beg	begin or beginning
CC	Contrast Color
cm	centimeter
dec	decrease or decreasing
gm	gram(s)
inc	increase or increasing
k	knit
p	purl
psso	pass slipped stitch over
M	marker
MC	Main Color
mm	milimeter
PM	place marker
psso	pass slipped stitch over
rem	remain or remaining
rep	repeat
rnd	round
sl	slip
st	stitch
sts	stitches
St st	Stocking stitch
tbl	through back loop
tog	together
yds	yards
yo	yarn over
yrn	yarn forward and around needle

SYMBOLS & TERMS

* or #   work instructions following or between * or # as many more times as indicated in addition to the first time.

( ) or [ ]   work enclosed instructions as many times as specified by the number immediately following **or** work all enclosed instructions in the stitch or space indicated **or** contains explanatory remarks

-   the number(s) given after a hyphen at the end of a row or round denote(s) the number of stitches or spaces you should have on that row or round.

KNIT TERMINOLOGY

UNITED STATES		INTERNATIONAL
gauge	=	tension
bind off	=	cast off

Yarn Weight Symbol & Names	SUPER FINE 1	FINE 2	LIGHT 3	MEDIUM 4	BULKY 5	SUPER BULKY 6	JUMBO 7
Type of Yarns in Category	Sock, Fingering Baby	Sport, Baby	DK, Light Worsted	Worsted, Afghan Aran	Chunky, Craft, Rug	Super Bulky, Roving	Jumbo, Roving
Knit Gauge Range in Stockinette St to 4" (10 cm)	27-32 sts	23-26 sts	21-24 sts	16-20 sts	12-15 sts	7-11 sts	6 sts and fewer
Advised Needle Size Range	1 to 3	3 to 5	5 to 7	7 to 9	9 to 11	11 to 17	17 and larger

*GUIDELINES ONLY: The chart above reflects the most commonly used gauges and needle sizes for specific yarn categories.

■▭▭▭ BEGINNER	Projects for first-time knitters using basic knit and purl stitches. Minimal shaping.
■■▭▭ EASY	Projects using basic stitches, repetitve stitch patterns, simple color changes, and simple shaping and finishing.
■■■▭ INTERMEDIATE	Projects with a variety of stitches, such as basic cables and lace, simple intarsia, double-pointed needles and knitting in the round needle techniques, mid-level shaping and finishing.
■■■■ EXPERIENCED	Projects using advanced techniques and stitches, such as short rows, fair isle, more intricate intarsia, cables, lace patterns and numerous color changes.

KNITTING NEEDLES

U.S.	50	35	19	17	15	13	11	----	----	10.5	10	9	8	7	6	5	4	3	----	2	1	0	----
U.K.	---	----	----	----	000	00	0	1	2	3	4	5	6	7	8	9	----	10	11	12	13	14	15
Metric mm	25	19	15	12.75	10	9	8	7.5	7	6.5	6	5.5	5	4.5	4	3.75	3.5	3.25	3	2.75	2.25	2	1.75

Casting On

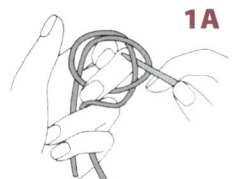 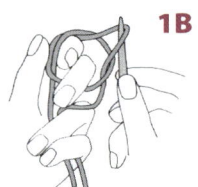  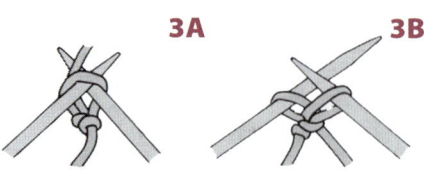

1A. Make a slip knot: Loop the yarn as shown and slip needle under the lower strand of the loop.
1B. Pull up a loop of yarn.

2. Pull the yarn end attached to the ball of yarn to tighten the slip knot leaving the other end approx. 4" [10 cm] long. Transfer needle to left hand.

3A. Insert the right-hand needle through slip knot and wind yarn over right-hand needle.
3B. Pull loop through slip knot.

4. Place new loop on left-handle needle. (You now have 2 stitches (sts) on your left-hand needle.)

5. Insert right-hand needle between last 2 stitches (sts) on left-hand needle and wind yarn over right-hand needle.

6. Pull loop through. Place this new loop on left-hand needle beside last stitch (st). (You now have 1 more stitch on left-hand needle.) Repeat (rep) steps 5 and 6 until required number of stitches (sts) have been cast on left-hand needle.

The Knit Stitch

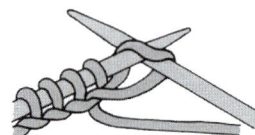  

1. Hold the needle with cast on stitches (sts) in your left hand, and the loose yarn attached to the ball at the back of work. Insert right-hand needle from left to right through the front of the first stitch (st) on the left-hand needle.

2. Wind the yarn from left to right over the point of the right-hand needle.

3. Draw the yarn through this original stitch (st) which forms a new stitch (st) on right-hand needle.

 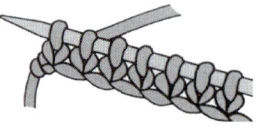

4. Slip the original stitch (st) off the left-hand needle, keeping the new stitch (st) on the right-hand needle.

5. To knit a row, repeat steps 1 to 4 until all stitches (sts) have been transferred from left-hand needle to right-hand needle. Turn the work by transferring the needle with stitches (sts) into your left hand to knit the next row.

The Purl Stitch

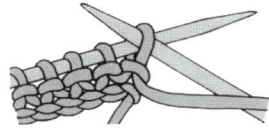  

1. With yarn at front of work, insert right-hand needle from right to left through front of first stitch (st) on left-hand needle.

2. Wind yarn around right-hand needle. Pull yarn through stitch (st).

3. Slip original stitch (st) off needle. Repeat (rep) these steps until all stitches (sts) on left-hand needle have been transferred onto right-hand needle to complete one row of purling.

Increasing and Decreasing

  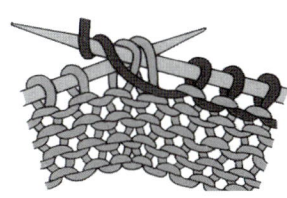

Increase 1 stitch (st) in next stitch (st): Work into front and back of stitch (st) as follows: Knit stitch (st), then before slipping it off needle, twist right-hand needle behind left-hand needle and knit again into back of loop. Slip original stitch (st) off needle. There are now 2 stitches (sts) on right-hand needle made from original stitch.

K2tog Decrease: Knit 2 stitches (sts) together (tog) through the front of both loops.

P2tog Decrease: Purl 2 stitches (sts) together (tog) through the front of both loops.

Casting Off

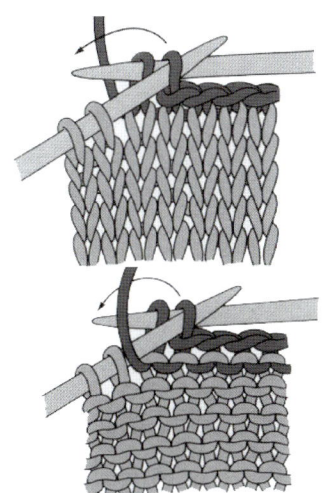

Cast off using knit stitch (knitwise): Knit the first 2 stitches (sts). *Using left-hand needle, lift first stitch (st) over second stitch (st) and drop it off between points of the 2 needles. Knit the next stitch (st); repeat (rep) from * until all stitches (sts) from left-hand needle have been worked and only 1 stitch (st) remains on the right-hand needle. Cut yarn (leaving enough to sew in end) and thread cut end through stitch (st) on needle. Draw yarn up firmly to fasten off last stitch (st).

Cast off using purl stitch (purlwise): Purl first 2 stitches (sts). *Using left-hand needle, lift first stitch (st) over second stitch (st) and drop it off needle. Purl next stitch (st) as described for casting off knitwise.

Yarn Information

Projects in this book were made with different weight yarns.
Any brand of of the specified weight yarn may be used.
It is best to refer to yardage/meters when determining how many
balls or skeins to purchase. Remember, to arrive at the finished size,
it is the GAUGE/TENSION that is important, not the brand of yarn.

For your convenience, listed below are the specific yarn ranges used to create our photographed models.

Cozy Mariner's Blanket
Mary Maxim® Starlette®

Mitered Eyelet Blanket
Mary Maxim® Super Baby® Stripes

Honeycomb Blanket
Mary Maxim® Baby's Best®

Cable Patches Blanket
Mary Maxim® Marbles®

Baby Entrelac Blanket
Mary Maxim® Baby Ragg® Sport

Lace & Cables Blanket
Mary Maxim® Baby's Best®

Every effort has been made to have the directions contained in this
pattern accurate and complete; however, we cannot be responsible for
misinterpretation, variance or errors in workmanship of the individual.

Copyright © 2017 by Leisure Arts, Inc., 104 Champs Blvd., STE 100, Maumelle, AR 72113-6738, www.leisurearts.com. All rights reserved. This publication is protected under federal copyright laws. Reproduction or distribution of this publication or any other Leisure Arts publication, including publications which are out of print, is prohibited unless specifically authorized. This includes, but is not limited to, any form of reproduction or distribution on or through the Internet, including posting, scanning or e-mail transmission.